BENEATH THE WILLOW

A WARRIOR'S JOURNEY THROUGH WOUNDS

LOUIS OROZCO LOPEZ

ACKNOWLEDGMENT

Thank you to those who shared a candle in the darkest of nights, to those who shared moments when time was running out, and finally, to those who shared the wisdom of the willow tree.

DEDICATION

"For those like I who have been lost and are still searching for a path..."

TABLE OF CONTENTS

Acknowledgment.. 1

Dedication... 2

Awaking: Roots & Steel.. 3

Chapter 1: Flames & Pain.. 4

Chapter 2: Choice & Promises................................. 10

Chapter 3: Ku & Ko.. 18

Chapter 4: Challenges & Why.................................. 23

Chapter 5: Trauma & Greif....................................... 30

Chapter 6: Paths & Procrastinating........................... 35

Chapter 7: Honour & Life.. 39

Chapter 8: Life & Death.. 47

Chapter 9: Mountains & Shoulders........................... 52

Chapter 10: Time & Growth....................................... 58

In Memory Of.. 61

About the Author... 62

零

AWAKENING: ROOTS & STEEL

Liu sat at the base of the great Willow and wept for he had become lost. His grief roiled and raged inside until he could bare the pain no more. In fury he drew his blade and cursed all things aloud. With rage filling his stomach he slashed and hacked at the dancing branches before him.

The Willow stood firm yet yielding, strong and supple as she had stood for over one hundred years. Pain filled her core, as the warrior's tears watered the ground beneath her subtle embrace.

FLAMES & PAIN

The willow tree danced in the soft breeze, its branches moving with the invisible ebb and flow of all things. Lui's mother had brought him here just as she had done on each of his birthdays before this.

Standing on the outskirts of their small village, they stood in front of the tree known to this quiet place as Yanagi.

Yanagi was rooted deep, yet she bent towards the setting sun. Half of her thousands of mighty arms danced above the lake, some tickling the surface and sending ripples into the cold sapphire blue as far as the eye could see. The other half of her arms thrashed and swayed like whips of wind over the gnarled roots that sank deep into the red dirt earth beneath them.

Lui's mother's face was calm, soft, and beautiful. Her eyes were as green as the forest that surrounded them, and her skin shone like the setting sun over the lake. Not only was she kind, but she was wise beyond her years, and each day she made it her sole purpose to teach Lui all that she could.

Today, they sat side by side as they had done so many times before, watching and listening to Yanagi, her branches now swaying gently like the softest of whispers on the wind.

"Life is the simple choice to live, Lui," she said softly. "Bend, but do not break."

Lui nodded silently. He had heard what his mother said, but he was not sure if he truly understood her. He was busy watching his mother's smile—a smile that stretched high on her face but somehow didn't quite reach her eyes.

Lui watched her emerald eyes as shadows gathered around them. She was tired, he could tell, and Lui knew it had been a long day. Though he knew this, and though he saw the shadows, he did not yet understand what lurked deep beneath the calm mask his mother so often wore.

There had been times when Lui had glimpsed the deep sorrow that showed itself as a single tear drop. He had seen how hard she fought to remain still despite her restlessness. As always, Lui listened while his mother spoke. The rest of the evening blurred into the night, and time passed as it always had and always would.

Some days later, on a cold morning, Lui raced home after forgetting his calligraphy brushes. It was early, and mist hung in the air as it crept inland, settling to sleep—a soft blanket covering the village.

Their humble house was silent. His mother must have left. Lui raced into his room, grabbed his brushes, and rushed towards the door. He stopped outside his mother's door—it was slightly ajar. Knowing his mother would likely reprimand his forgetfulness, and accepting this, he called his mother's name and walked into her room, asking for a hug before he left for school.

What he expected to hear was her irritated lecture on how if he slowed down, he wouldn't forget, how if he focused on one thing he would remember, how if Lui put as much effort into this world as he did staring up at the clouds, he would be a great man someday.

Silence hung in the room. Lui's mother lay still in bed, motionless, her dark eyes empty. She clutched a small stitched bear. A gentle breeze pushed sheets of pastel-coloured papers around the room—paper inked with words he could not read.

Moving the papers into a pile, Lui approached the stillness that was his mother. Her face still bore the softest of smiles, but her body was utterly motionless. The truth cut him like a blade—his mother had chosen to leave him. There was no sickness, no dark figure robed in black, no bright lights, just his mother's body, her decision, and Lui's fear.

At first, terror engulfed him. But quickly, something darker roiled beneath the surface. After standing still for far too long, Lui turned his back on the only family he had and began to walk.

Rage, wrath, and resentment gave birth to hatred. With each step he took, the anger grew. His heart was heavy as a stone, and somewhere inside of him, an emptiness was born. His fists hurt—they were clenched so tight, but not a single tear touched his cheeks. He couldn't feel; he refused to allow the pain erupting inside him to break free. He began falling, tumbling inside himself deeper and deeper. At first, he feared the impact. Soon, he would hit the floor of himself, his bones would break, and his body would shatter, but he... he would not quit. He would not run from the pain of living. He would not take the coward's path out. Lui hated her for what she had done, for leaving him alone, and so he opened his eyes and embraced the ghost of his old life, for he knew nothing would ever be the same again.

Lui refused to cry, and yet the emptiness threatened to swallow him whole.

Knowing that Lui's mother had taken her own life cast her memory into shame. The villagers offered soft smiles of sympathy, but as they did, they whispered behind his back. It was as if, by leaving, she had cast him into shadow, and somehow Lui sensed he would spend the rest of his life trying to lift the weight of her dishonour.

Lui couldn't comprehend the choice his mother had made; he just didn't understand how anyone or anything could choose death over life.

Time passed, and Lui returned to Yanagi, the tree that had offered him shade from the sun and shelter from the rain. Perhaps now it could shelter him from his own pain.

Sitting there alone beneath Yanagi felt different. The peaceful sound of wind rustling through the dancing branches somehow now felt chaotic. Lui's heart began to thunder—drowning out all peace within him.

In desperation, Lui closed his eyes, willing the memory of her into his mind, but all that remained were shards. His mother was a shattered mirror; the pure reflection she once cast was gone.

Desperately, Lui clutched at the fragments, longing to see her one last time—if only to say goodbye. Yet, the more he reached for her face, the less he could see. The only shard left was a promise: a memory of his mother just days before her death. They had sat beneath this very tree, her gaze so fierce it made him shrink.

"*Promise me, Lui,*" she had said, her voice a fierce whisper. "*Promise me you will live twice the life you are destined for. Be stronger than fate, stronger than anything I could ever teach you. Be stronger than me!*"

All Lui could do was nod, as the fragments shattered over and over, leaving nothing but echoes. Now, with her gone, that promise bore down on him, crushing him, crushing the fragile pieces of him to dust... but he would not break!

No, he would not break; he would not bend, as she had taught him. Instead, he would let his anger harden him, like a stone crushed by insurmountable pressure.

Lui vowed to keep that promise, but not for her—no, for himself. He would live twice the life he was meant to, not out of honour, but out of defiance. For to bend meant understanding, and he could never understand why she had left him.

His fists clenched as a cold resolve took root deep inside his heart. Lui would grow stronger. Harder. Colder.

The boy who had once sat beneath the Yanagi had died with his mother.

Now all that remained was Lui, sat alone beneath the willow tree, a forge fire of pain, molten, red, and raw. Not only did it fuel Lui, it became him.

"NO AMOUNT OF FORCE CAN BREAK THE WIND; IT MAY BEND, SHIFT, OR SLOW, BUT THE WIND'S VERY ESSENCE IS TO REFUSE STILLNESS."

— YANAGI

CHOICE & PROMISES

As the weeks passed, Lui knew nothing would ever be the same. In the days and weeks that followed his mother's death, Lui found himself visiting more and more relatives—some for a day or two, some for a week. Eventually, though, Lui found himself standing before a rather large set of ornate carved wooden gates.

It was a little after sunrise, and a family member whose name Lui had refused to learn had dropped him here in the middle of nowhere. The gate loomed in front of him as if it were some sort of symbol.

"*Where are we going?*" Lui had asked in an uninterested, flat tone.

"*Those doors can be one of two things,*" the nameless relative said over his shoulder, his voice old and frail.

"*They can serve as a barrier, trapping you within your past, or they could be gateways to the next chapter in your life.*"

With that, he turned his back and walked down the dusty lane, leaving the words hanging in the air for Lui to either listen to or ignore.

The heavy Hinoki doors swung open as a lean, tall man that Lui did not recognise slowly walked towards him. The stranger wore a long robe, his head shaved like a monk, but the darkness in the man's eyes was far from the peaceful gaze of the monks from Lui's village.

It wasn't long before Lui realised he had found a different kind of relative—one whose eyes didn't speak of softness and calm but of wrath and menace. The man before him would not yield; no matter the size of the mountain, this man would simply climb high!

Ondori was a distant uncle who ran a dojo in the heart of Kumano. Within the walls of Ondori's dojo, locked behind those giant gates, were hundreds of years of experience. Ondori made no attempt to appease or reassure Lui when discussing his future with him.

"*Train, eat, sleep and grow, or you may go to the kitchen and feed those who dare to grow.*" Ondori stated calmly and simply.

Lui realised he was about to make a decision that would change the rest of his life. Pausing, he thought about how his life had been forced in this direction. How his mother's actions and the actions of others had left him here on the doorstep of his own decision.

Ondori took one knee, his cold grey eyes meeting Lui's, no smile curling his lipsas he spoke, "*What is it you want from your life, Lui?*"

Lui could not answer; it could not be explained. It simply was. So Lui said the only thing he could think of, "*To live tenfold!*"

十倍生きる

His uncle wasted no time; the moment the outer doors closed behind Lui, Ondori pointed to one of many doors at the far side of a large square.

"*Start at the first door on the far left, knock, introduce yourself, and do what you are told. If you make it to the last door, you may stay!*"

Lui stared up at his uncle's stern face, biting back a hundred questions as he started towards the first door.

At the first door, Lui knelt just outside, softly announcing himself, as was the polite thing to do, ***"Shitsureishimasu!"***

The door slid open, and a kind-faced elderly woman poked her head out. Her hair was grey and tied back, her wrinkles deep, and in one hand, she clutched a book, her thumb carefully holding her place.

"*I am June; you may call me Baa-chan, everybody else does!*" she said with a mischievous wink.

"*Come in, we have things to do, and the day is already tired!*" Lui simply nodded and did as he was told.

Baa-chan was kind, soft and sweet, and it quickly became apparent to Lui that she was the opposite of his uncle.

Pouring tea into a cup, Baa-chan said with a ceremonious air, "*I am the eldest of things; in this place, my wisdom is used to decide if you are capable of learning.*" The tea steamed as it sat in the small cups.

"Drink!" Baa-chan said the moment she finished setting the teapot down. Lui raised the cup to his mouth and softly blew across the surface, then he drank.

"*This is the first and last drink I will offer you; from here on out, you will drink only water. Do you understand?*"

Lui nodded, savouring the remaining sips in the small cup.

"*Good, you may leave. Come back to me if you're ever hurt,*" Baa-chan said with a warm smile.

So Lui set down the cup, offered his respects, and proceeded to the next door. Each door Lui passed through was stranger than the last, a series of small things, each as important as the last and, in its own way, fundamental in understanding before the next door could be entered.

As Lui progressed down the doors, the clarity of the lesson subtly conveyed became apparent. At the fifth door, Lui was invited in only if he took a razor from the occupier and shaved his own head before entering. Without question, Lui did.

The seventh door found Lui changing into new clothes, a simple robe and trousers before he was allowed to leave.

The ninth door was, if anything, the strangest yet. Lui was greeted by a young, stout-looking man covered from head to foot in black text and symbols. Writings covered his bald head and his bare feet. Lui nodded as the man gestured towards a seating area with inks and needles set out.

Lui knew this to be Tebori, but surely he was too young—far too young to be tattooed.

Lui left the ninth door, having endured what seemed to be countless hours of inkless needle pricks. Without so much as a word from the man who tapped rhythmically onto the bamboo, forcing the needle into his flesh. After a long while had passed and the sun had started to set, abruptly the man stopped. Pointing to the door, he said,

"*You may go to the last door; do not come back to me until you know what it is I put onto your skin.*"

The last door opened onto a large living area. Lui was unsure who opened the door, as the room was empty. Sleeping mats and packs lay across the floor in neat rows. The silence of the room broke as a door to the rear slid open, and countless faces, young and old, burst into the silence; not one of them looked in his direction.

The room was utter chaos, a hive of activity, and then one by one, they each climbed into a bedroll. Appearing from nowhere, Ondori addressed the room,

"*This is my nephew Lui, and now he is your brother. Show him as you were shown and fetch him a roll and clothes for tomorrow.*"

The remainder of the night was a blur, and the next morning, Lui was thrown into a relentless schedule. The days started at sunrise and ended as darkness covered the training square in shadow.

The throbbing tightness of freshly bruised skin became normal; his legs screamed in agony every night as he lay down, and his hands physically twitched from the relentless drills. He was not alone in this pain, but he was still very much alone.

When Lui struggled to keep pace with the others, a dark fire began to burn deep within him; every misstep and every failure only stoked Lui's rage. Refusing to cry when the overwhelming emotions swelled in him like a giant uncontrollable wave, Lui chose to fight on.

Refusing to show any sign of weakness or emotion, Lui simply bit down hard and sunk deeper and deeper inside himself. Like a rock falling into a pond, he found his innermost depths, and there he remained.

"*Strength is earned through hardship,*" his uncle declared, eyes cold and unyielding. *"The sword becomes sharp only after being tempered by fire."*

Lui disagreed, for he was no sword; he was a rock, but day after day, week after week, and month after month, the young man that rock was slowly shaped by the unseen currents of consistency.

Lui's body began growing stronger, more flexible, and more skilled. He learned to adapt, he learned to overcome and outsmart. Where his strength or stamina failed, he wielded rage. The other students had taken to calling him Oni, while his uncle simply nodded at Lui's progress. He offered no praise, only the harsh reminder that true strength comes from purpose, not from anger.

Deep inside the repetition of Lui's new life, he found an escape from the burden of his vow—to live twice the life he was destined for.

Twice the strength, twice the power, twice the rage, twice the weapon. Though he still failed often and had much to learn, Lui decided that from now on, when he collected his Bokken, he would take two—one for him and one for his mother.

From the moment Lui's fingers wrapped around those hilts, Lui became something other than flesh and bone; he became Niten Oni.

"LET YOUR WHY
BE THE STORM—
BEND IF YOU
MUST, BUT NEVER
BREAK."

— YANAGI

三

KU & KO

Just like the walls of the dojo, Lui kept the secrets, the things he couldn't show the world, at bay. This place had its own synergy, its own force, and so did Lui; he was fuelled by something more.

This inner strength often collided headfirst with the way of the dojo, crashing into the code and shattering the standard. Sometimes it was for the better, but more often than not, it was for the worse.

Each day presented a new test of skill or endurance, and sometimes it required both. Despite Lui's apparent inherited strength and speed, he usually finished at the top in bouts of strength and intellect, and often in the top ten for stamina and speed. Lui always completed every task, even where many failed. Lui began to feel increasingly like an outcast. Failure was lonely, but success was solitude.

It was one such silent and lonely night that Lui met Kaito, one of his uncle's students.

Kaito was a little older than Lui but not by much. He moved with purpose and yet somehow remained graceful. Kaito looked as if he belonged in the dojo and had been there his whole life.

Lui's and Kaito's ethos were complete opposites. Where Lui saw black, Kaito saw white. Simply put, the two were perfect enemies, but in a rare twist of circumstance, they became thick friends.

Often, their paths crossed head-on in the dojo. Despite the chaos that usually followed, and though it took some time, the two always managed to accept that they were, in fact, well-suited as opposing forces.

One winter, after a particularly cold and demanding mountain run that lasted from sunrise to sunset, Lui sat alone on the roof of the sleeping quarters. This place had become a favourite spot of Lui's, allowing him to see the entire dojo, and yet with the slightest upward tilt of his gaze, he would be transported to an endless realm of darkness and stars.

Lui was angry, his negative thoughts smashing into his mind. He had finished the run—yes, that was all that was required of him. Yet still, he brooded, furious with himself for not having finished first.

It wasn't long before Kaito softly sat beside him, legs crossed on the parapet of the gentle slope of the roof. Kaito had finished second but still seemed pleased with himself, as evidenced by his bright and wide smile, with no frown or worry across his face.

"You're too hard on yourself," Kaito said, giving Lui a reassuring pat on the back. *"We all fail. It's part of life."*

Lui frowned. *"Fail? I did not fail. I finished; I just did not finish where I wanted to!"*

"Then you failed, but that is okay. Had you wanted to finish where you finished, you would have succeeded," Kaito said with a warm smile. *"... but you wanted first, and so even though you finished, you failed."*

Lui frowned. *"Did you not fail? Did you not seek to be the fastest? The best?"*

Kaito mused, *"I sought only to complete the task, having given it my best effort!"*

Kaito paused, the night sky hanging on his every word. *"There is no such thing as failure, unless, of course, you want to fail!"*

Kaito answered quickly, as if he had already anticipated the question. *"Not if I lived a good life, for that is my path, and everyone has their own path to walk, their own story to tell!"*

Although Lui didn't ask any more questions that night, nor did he tell Kaito what he thought of his opinion, he decided right then and there that he would never forget those words or this conversation.

From then on, Lui strove to question Kaito after every event, seeking wisdom where his own failed him. In doing so, Lui found that the more he reflected on his own choices, the wiser he became.

It wasn't long before Lui started to value not only victory but failure too. For in failure, there was still a path to success, should he choose to continue; and by continuing, Lui now truly believed there could be no failure.

The harder the days became, the deeper their friendship rooted. The two pushed each other beyond their own limits, and in time, both finished ahead of the rest of the dojo in most areas. Where they did not finish first, they accepted the fact, analysed their strategy, made adjustments, planned, reanalysed, and then prepared for their next opportunity.

"THERE IS NO SUCH THING AS FAILURE, UNLESS, OF COURSE, YOU WANTED TO FAIL. THEN YOUR JOURNEY IS COMPLETE."

— KAITO

四

CHALLENGES & WHY

The dojo was a place of escape. Everything that did not belong was left behind those ornate doors. This space was sacred; it was for focus and disciplined work. Amid the clank of folded steel, the rhythmic movements of calm were hard to spot—unless, of course, you were not looking, and then the calm felt natural. It belonged here as much as the sound of bare skin against smooth wood.

Moments of calm were considered a great honour, as they required immense awareness to recognise stillness while maintaining steady breathing and instinctive movements that allowed the calm to flow naturally. Any deliberate attempt to achieve it only led to frustration. Though moments of calm became a regular occurrence between Liu and his sensei, it wasn't until these moments stretched into minutes that he began to feel a deeper connection to his training, as if the stillness was becoming part of him.

Knowing Liu could not stay at the dojo forever, he made every effort to absorb everything.

Right now, Liu was like a sponge in a bucket of water, but the true test of his mastery would be how much water he could retain when he was removed from the bucket.

Ondori, Liu's sensei, was a renowned samurai known by many who fought alongside him in the last war as "*Ondori the Last,*" for he was always the last one to draw his blade, the last one off the battlefield, and the last thing many saw.

His renown and deep desire to pass on his experience made him more than just a teacher. Ondori embodied a true understanding that extended beyond the way of the sword, speaking often of balance—not only in combat but in all things.

Liu was taught to find harmony within himself. Despite the unsettling molten pit deep within him, he was able to display both strength and softness, discipline and understanding.

"*One cold winter evening, as they trained in the dojo, Ondori spoke to Liu.* The words echoed in him, and Liu knew they would stay.

'A true warrior,' Ondori said, guiding Liu through deliberate movements, 'understands the importance of compassion. Strength without empathy is a burden.' Ondori paused, as if reflecting on his own words, then added, ***'There can be no victory without peace, for peace is balance!'***

As Liu pondered his sensei's words, understanding seemed to bridge one idea to another. Liu's mind lit up with new insights from past lessons.

Many grueling days of training followed, and Liu's will to fight, to live, to learn remained as strong as the day he arrived. But soon, the day of his final test came.

Though most students referred to it as a test, it was more of an undertaking. Students were required to display, demonstrate, or deliver proof that they had understood one key lesson from Sensei Ondori.

Some fasted for days, others climbed mountains, while others forged blades. Very few passed, and even fewer were given the honour and right to leave the school, wearing the colours of the dojo.

Liu arrived at the main tatami empty-handed, no sword hung at his waist. Barefoot and dressed in his simple, well-worn fudangi, he stood among other students who wore formal kamishimo, each decorated with a perfectly cared-for katana.

With Sensei Ondori kneeling before all his senior students, he asked each one in turn to demonstrate their understanding. There was no indication of pass or fail; Ondori did not move an inch. He simply called a name, bowed, and watched as his students jumped to their feet, eager to impress. Some slashed at rolled tatami mats, others demonstrated katas, and others spoke of their deep understanding of the lessons they had been taught.

When Liu's name was called by Ondori, Liu bowed low and spoke, with his head still bowed.

"*Sensei Ondori, here I kneel before you, as ready to learn now as on the day I entered this dojo. If I spoke of true understanding, it would be a lie, for such a truth must surely take a lifetime to achieve...*"

Liu paused, thinking, for this was not a rehearsed speech—he spoke simply from his heart.

"*A lifetime of experiences, of failures and successes, a lifetime of striving to know more, for I believe that though I am your student, I am also a student of all things, including myself.*"

Another pause, longer than the last, while Liu searched for the right words. "*And to truly understand and embody all you have taught, to do this, I must find my own answers to the very questions your lessons have forced me to ask.*"

Liu remained low, his eyes now closed, knowing he was not the last to be tested.

Ondori rose silently and walked over to Liu, taking a katana from the wall next to a painting of a willow tree. He placed the sword in front of Liu.

"*This sword was your mother's. Though she fought as often with her words and fists as with her blade, it was placed upon that wall the day she told me she could not fight with so much love in her heart. Now, Liu, the blade is yours. This dojo is proud to have you wear our colours.*"

Later that night, Ondori and Liu shared tea as they discussed Liu's plans to travel. Deep in thought and easy conversation, they did not notice how late it had become when a messenger arrived for Ondori. The messenger, dressed in plain clothes and a worn cloak, appeared tired from his long journey. As was polite, Ondori offered him a seat, rest, and something to drink. At first, the messenger refused, but Ondori simply asked, "*Will you return without delay to the place from which you brought this message?*"

The messenger replied honestly, "*Yes, for I will receive payment upon proving the message was delivered.*"

Ondori paused for a moment before insisting, "*Then sit, rest, and drink. I will write you a reply, so you have proof, though I sense your word is well respected.*"

On the man's heavy cloak shone the unmistakable royal seal. This messenger was no ordinary runner; he was a royal courier.As Liu watched his uncle unroll the scroll, he followed the movement of his eyes down the parchment. Ondori looked up and asked Liu to fetch him ink and a brush.

The messenger and Liu sat in silence for some time as Ondori drafted a simple, short reply. Once completed, he laid the scroll out to dry, using stones to pin the parchment to the floor.

"*When you deem the ink dry enough to resume your journey, you have my leave to deliver my response,*" Ondori whispered.

Liu looked down, somewhat at a loss for words when he read the simple response Ondori had written: ***"With Honour."***

Looking up at his sensei, Liu asked simply, "*A challenge from the emperor, now, at your age – why?*"

Ondori's response, spoken from the heart, was as simple as his written words. "*The emperor's 'why' is not my 'why.' There is only one 'why' that matters – my own. For we can walk but one path. The path I chose long ago is decided by my 'why.' It is my 'why' that speaks to my heart, telling me that the path I now step onto is one of my choosing. So ask me again, Liu.*"

Liu considered for a while before asking, "*Why do you choose to accept, when it could mean grave injury or even death?*"

Ondori smiled wide, almost ear to ear. "*Now you are asking the right questions.*" He gave a slight laugh as he continued, "*In time, perhaps... yes, perhaps one day you will understand my 'why,' though you should not waste your time figuring out mine. It is your own 'why' that is important.*"

Frustrated with the cryptic response, Liu asked again, ***"But why?"***

Ondori smiled, this time with sorrow and softness written clearly across his face. "*Honour. My 'why' is my own honour, for without this, I am nothing more than a thug. So perhaps the emperor wishes to challenge me, wishes me dead, believes I have wronged him. If this is the case, only my honour can clear my name... and by refusing to fight, I lose my honour.*"

Liu was not there to see Ondori fall in battle. He was not there to witness his uncle's last moments—the man who had taken him in. He was not there for the one person who accepted his presence, and this filled him with rage, deep inside, adding to the pile of roaring red coals. He had done as Ondori had asked, Liu had left to find his own 'why'.'

It was only after many months that Liu finally heard the news of Ondori's fate. Even though he had suspected what might happen, the confirmation that Ondori had fallen during the challenge still shook him to his core. The loss hit him harder than he had expected, leaving him to grapple with the grief and unanswered questions it raised.

With the loss of their sensei, the dojo sent messages to the top five students of Master Ondori, requesting they return to continue his teachings. Though Liu answered the messenger, he did not return home, for now, as he travelled again, he found he felt no place was his home.

Liu's life continued while so many around him had not—his mother, his friends, his teacher. With each death, Liu felt with greater intensity the need to continue, to do more, to be more.

"WHEN WALKING
THROUGH A FOREST
FILLED WITH WOLVES,
THE REASON YOU ENTER
MUST BE GREATER THAN
THE WOLVES' HUNGER,
GREATER THAN YOUR
OWN FEAR. OTHERWISE,
YOU RISK BECOMING
LOST AMIDST THE TREES,
AND FOOD FOR THE
WOLVES."

— YANAGI

五

TRAUMA & GREIF

The battlefield now lay as silent as a graveyard; chaos slept upon a blanket of blood. War—a tapestry of guilt and despair, a canvas of victory painted with the heavy, coppery taste of death.

Memories of friends now smashed into broken pieces of reality—broken pieces of regret.

There is no glory in death, no honour in war, no pride to be had from taking dreams and destroying life; and yet, as warriors, as samurai, they did what must be done.

Liu wandered through the carnage, utterly lost, overwhelmed by grief as he sorted friend from foe. The faces of his fallen companions, once shining with laughter and love, now lay slick and still in the mud.

Already, the white vultures circled above. Overwhelming sorrow cascaded down Liu's soul, for he knew a part of him would never be the same. Though he lived, his soul was dying—a spluttering candle in the wind.

Of all the faces he saw, half cast in pain and half cast in shock, Haruto's face haunted him the most.

One of Liu's dearest friends, Haruto, was always bright and spirited, bubbling over with infectious laughter. Many who knew Haruto called him Happy, for joy was truly in his heart. Haruto was a constant source of morale, support and comfort to those who knew him.

Happy carried with him a small tin tub. When questioned by Liu about what it was, Happy simply answered, ***"It's my Heorte."***

A tin heart—a simple container Haruto kept mementos inside. Happy memories and moments he didn't want to forget.

Liu stood by a small shrine—not a grave; Haruto did not want a grave; he only wanted to be free from containment and for a place to be remembered.

Haruto's absence was not only painful; it was crushing, as yet another one of Liu's loved ones had left him here in this place.

Haruto's ***"Heorte"*** had been fondly tended when the battlefield had been cleared. Its contents—a collection of notes and images—told stories or stirred memories.

Haruto had often spoken of his tin heart with a smile, saying, *"Even in the darkest times, we must hold onto joy. For old age and darkness will one day take everything from us."*

Liu had never fully grasped this ideology until now—a way of remembering what mattered most when the darkness they all knew and felt was too much or their age took from them the last of their happiness.

The tin, filled with small joys, seemed absurd in the face of Liu's overwhelming grief.

Wrapped deep within a shawl of sorrow, Liu thought long and hard about Haruto's words. Heorte was more than an old word; it was a way of life. Despite the crushing weight of the world, Haruto had found a way to cling to moments of joy.

Though this remarkably simple thing brought a smile to Liu's face, he felt emptiness deep within him—burning, fueling his life.

Kneeling now, months after the bloodshed, thick blacks and reds had been consumed by the ground, replaced by lush green hues. Liu placed Haruto's box into a small hole he had dug in the earth with his bare hands. As he covered it with fistfuls of mud, Liu pondered the final gift a dear friend had left behind. Wordless wisdom lay now buried in Haruto's box.

Over the next few weeks and months, as Liu continued to live, his grief and anger were as heavy as a brewing storm cloud. Despite the internal struggle, he began to seek out the small moments of joy in each day.

It was not ignorance or refusal to accept reality; it was as simple as looking into the dark night sky, eyes searching for that first glowing star. It was hope.

Without knowing it, Haruto had changed Liu's life. This new way of thinking, this new mindset, was a powerful one.

Late at night, while Liu sought refuge in a sleeping world, his mind replayed images from within Haruto's box. Though buried in a shallow grave, the box's truths would never be forgotten.

Liu made sure he wouldn't forget, for with every death came a new promise: to live, to continue on for those who did not.

"IT'S HARD TO MOVE FORWARD WITHOUT LOOKING BACK!"

— HARUTO

六

PATHS & PROCRASTINATING

Liu travelled to far and distant lands. He climbed every mountain and ventured into every valley. He was not afraid, for he followed his heart, stopping when he became tired and eating when he became hungry.

With each new step, Liu found himself compelled to continue. It was as if he was pulled by an invisible chord, along an unseen road. The stillness of the world around him allowed his mind to talk to his innermost self.

"*Live more, go further, climb higher!*" the inner voice said with passion.

After countless days and nights, and more full moons than faces, Liu came across a peak that stretched high into the clouds. This was a mountain greater than any he had seen. Spending the night at the base of the great mountain, Liu weighed his options.

Walk around it. Turn back. Climb up. Three options, each as taxing as the last and each a journey in its own right. Climbing into his bedroll, Liu looked up at the mountain; he watched the sky as the heavens swept down the face of it and quilted the world around him. The cold, moist air helped cool his skin, for the day had been hot.

Liu would sleep on it, he decided, and then he lay back, closed his eyes, and rested.

Waking with the rising sun, Liu realised that the answer had not yet come to him, and so he decided to stay another day. Again, Liu pulled out his sleeping roll, grateful for the time to rest, for he had truly come many leagues. Again, just as the night before, the night sky fell soft as a blanket, wrapping Liu and helping him find peaceful sleep.

Liu rose with the sun, and still he had come to no decision, so he searched for fresh water and food, and time passed just as the sun arced through the sky, only to set behind the great mountain.

This happened time and time again until Liu lost count of the days he'd stood before the mountain, undecided.

Again Liu sat staring up at the mountain, his mind bouncing from one option to another. He was mentally drained from thinking, internally battling between the choices that he offered himself. At first, the choice seemed like a blessing, but as time went on, the choice became stressful and frustrating, for he did not know which way to go.

That night, Liu decided to toss a stone at the base of the mountain's slope; if it rolled back down, he would turn around.

If it rolled off to a side, he would go around, and if by some impossible chance it rolled uphill, he would climb the mountain.

The stone struck and instantly rolled back down the slope toward him. ***"Oh no!"*** Liu exclaimed to himself, "*turn back after all these many miles?*" It was in that moment he realised there had only ever been two options: go around or go over.

Would he stay at the base of the mountain until the two choices became one?

Picking up another stone, this time Liu decided to flip it in the air. If the pale side landed up, he would go around, and if the darker side landed up, he would go over.

The stone flipped high in the sky, spinning before landing in Liu's hand, pale side up.

"*Huh, I suppose I'll go around!*" Liu said with a smile on his face as he began to climb the mountain at last.

"CONSIDER THAT WHEREVER YOU STAND NOW WAS YOUR PATH ALL ALONG AND CONTINUE NOW TO WALK TOWARDS YOUR GOAL."

— YANAGI

七

HONOUR & LIFE

High above the mountain, lost within cumulus clouds, Liu sought shelter in a large cave. Exhausted as he was, this cave would at least provide some refuge from the elements while he waited for the sun to rise and warm his frozen skin.

The air was frigid, and the wind howled through the valley below, forcing its way up the face of the mountain and causing the cave mouth to howl like a wolf. Liu knew he had climbed well, and now he had to rest, for the hardest part was yet to come.

Climbing a mountain was tough, but descending after such a climb was not only challenging but treacherous. Lighting a small fire, Liu took some dried fish from his pack. Sitting there, drinking pine tea and eating smoked fish, he allowed himself to settle, both inside and out.

The relentless howl of the wind meant he most likely would not sleep well, but he had to allow his body to rest and recover before continuing.

Breathing he focused his mind on the howling windthat shifted and distorted in his ears.

Sitting almost as if in a trance, Liu noticed a flickering shadow moving on the cave wall. His hand moved slowly, with purpose, towards the hilt of his katana as a small flickering shape danced and distorted, growing larger and larger. At first glance, Liu could have sworn it was a small child's shadow, but as his hand raised to his waist, it flickered into a multi-headed thing with more limbs than he could count. As his fingers wrapped around the hilt, it melded into the rhythm of the flickering flames,huge and serpentine it approached him, muffled by the sound of the roaring winds.

In that moment, as Liu decided to draw his katana, he realised the howling wind was not the cause of the sound; in fact, the direction of the wind had switched and was now reverberating from behind him. Despite this, Liu remained calm, refusing to let fear force his hand. He waited until the shadow cast before him stretched onto the ceiling above.

Liu took a deep breath, and as he exhaled, his breath froze in the air before him. Without another moment's delay, he spun, drawing his sword as the creature fell upon him.

In one smooth motion, Liu drew and spun, kicking himself back as the thing before him, still shifting, fell upon his blade.

There was no blood, no sound—just giant eyes staring deep into Liu's innermost thoughts. The creature before him smiled within Liu's mind. One of its giant paws buried hilt-deep on Liu's katana. Neither spoke; neither moved. The giant serpent-like creature ruffled its wings and stared wildly at Liu.

"*AWWW! You splintered me with your death stick! Why would you do that? It hurt!*" The thing spat in Liu's face.

Scrambling back, Liu narrowly missed crawling into the fire. Getting to his feet, he stammered, "*You...you speak!*"

"*I spoke of your spike, yes!*" it grunted.

"*What...what are you?*" Liu managed.

"*What am I? What are you?*" it asked in a mocking tone.

Liu found a little more of his tongue, for he hadn't been eaten yet. "*I'm Liu who are you?*"

The creature seemed to delight in answering, "*I am the Yamawaro!*"

"*Yamawaro?*" Liu asked, confused.

"*Yes, that's right! Well done, you remembered, though it's only been a few seconds!*" Yamawaro sniggered as its talons clicked and clacked on the hard stone floor.

The monstrous thing continued, "*May I steal a piece of your fire?*"

Not sure what the creature meant, Liu nodded dumbly.

Yamawaro pulled his paw with a quick sharp yank and snatched it back—katana and all. It then stuck its paw directly into the fire behind Liu. Looking up, Liu counted immense scaled armour on Yamawaro's chest. Behind him, Liu now heard the sound of steel hissing as it melted. Bright white light filled the entire cave, and Liu shut his eyes for fear of being blinded.

"*No mortal has set foot in my cave in a millennia; why have you sought me out?*" Yamawaro asked as he removed his now-healed foot from the fire.

Still with his eyes closed, Liu simply said, "*I did not seek you out; I sought the shelter of your cave. I am sorry to disturb you, great one.*"

"*You didn't think I was so great when you stuck your metal thorn into my foot, did you?*" Yamawaro's voice echoed through Liu's mind.

"*I'm sorry! You looked so big; I was scared!*" Liu said, honesty clear in his voice.

"*No...no, you're still big. I'm still scared, but you're talking, so clearly you're not going to eat me just yet!*" Liu said, a little smile curling his lip.

"*So you think because I'm big and scary, I was going to eat you, but because I haven't eaten you yet, I'm not going to eat you at all? You make no sense!*" Yamawaro huffed. "*The first conversation I've had in a mortal age, and I get to speak to you, a fever-stuck madman filled with fear and rage!*"

Liu stared up at the creature. "*Fear and rage? What do you know of me, creature?*"

"*I know that your kind are weak, and your minds are weaker still!*" Yamawaro mocked.

"*People don't stumble into my home by chance; no, they must have a certain something deep within their core, something like your swords that needs burning out with sheer power!*" Yamawaro purred as it pawed at the embers of the fire that had begun to die out. It snorted, and the fire danced into life once more with renewed vigour.

"*As you have found me and made me laugh with your small mind, I will answer one question and give you one gift. You name it, and I will make it so!*"

Yamawaro said with flint-black eyes; so black, the fire disappeared within them.

"*My katana; it meant a lot to me. Can you bring it back, please, Yamawaro?*" asked Liu.

"*Give me your word you won't stick it into me again?*" Yamawaro chuckled.

"*Yes, I promise!*" No sooner said than Liu's katana—his mother's katana—was suddenly in his hand.

Liu placed the blade away. "*Thank you!*" he said.

"*You won't thank me later,*" Yamawaro said, "*when you realise you could have asked for her back instead! Your mind is stuck in grief and death when it should be living in love and life!*"

Liu felt instant rage flare up inside him; without realising it, he had stood.

"*You could have brought her back?*" he asked.

"*Perhaps. I wouldn't know; nobody ever asked for that. They always ask for something too quickly; they never take the time to ask a question first! You humans spend your lives searching, yet you find yourselves short of things to ask!*" Yamawaro giggled now like a small child.

Liu was just about to open his mouth when he realised he was being tricked into asking for things.

If he asked if Yamawaro could bring somebody back, it would not matter, for he couldn't force the creature to do so, having already foolishly rushed into asking for his blade and giving his word not to use the blade to harm the creature again!

"You're smarter than you look, tiny one. For your silence, I'll give you a gift, though you should know I am within your mind also; I hear your every thought!"

As if to prove a point, without moving his dragon-like mouth, Yamawaro told Liu his blade would never melt again, for it had been reforged from magic.

After a long silence that stretched into the night, Liu asked, "*As I have failed to bring her back, them all back, how do I live a life enough to honour them?*"

Yamawaro looked at Liu with pity in his eyes. "*My dear tiny thing, for one so fierce, brave, and strong, you have missed so much! You have hidden yourself from love and pain and armoured yourself in rage and anger. To honour those who died, you simply have to live, and within you, they now live too!*"

The fire crackled and spat hot coals as a phantom wind blew through the mouth of the cave. Swirls of smoke and ash stung Liu's eyes, and by the time he brushed the offending debris out of them, Yamawaro was gone.

Liu's katana lay, its tip buried in the red-hot coals. At first, Liu thought it was some sort of vision, but as he stared at the blade of his katana, he saw reflected in the shaft the shape of a mighty creature getting smaller and smaller as it eventually disappeared into the mirror within his blade.

There was no mistaking it. The cave was filled with light, and Liu felt rested, though he could not shake the feeling of some otherworldly presence. He packed up his things and headed for the entrance of the cave. As he left, Liu turned to the mountain cave and shouted into the depths, ***"Thank you!"***

Liu smiled as he heard the same words echoed back.

"TO HONOUR THOSE WHO DIED, YOU SIMPLY HAVE TO LIVE, AND WITHIN YOU THEY NOW LIVE TOO!"

— HARUTO

八

LIFE & DEATH

Travelling through a vast forest of towering trees, Liu watched the shadows form dark shapes around him. Walking with purpose, occasionally stepping over a gnarled root or ducking around a twisted vine, Liu listened to the gentle rustling of the leaves. As he listened, he found his thoughts were calm and still, hushed by the whispers of the forest. His journey into the cave had been by chance, but here Liu chose his path, each step picked with greater care and attention than the last.

As Liu moved deeper into the forest, the sun dimmed, though it was far from night. A thick and heavy mist seemed to gradually grow like saplings from the ground; the mist reached up and up towards the canopy of trees. Though the fog tried to be free from its own weight, it was too dense to escape the soil's grasp and instead hung around Liu like a shroud.

It was here in the dimness of the wood that Liu saw him—the man whose face he knew he would not forget.

An old man, with wispy long grey hair, hunched over with age, wrinkled hands clutching a tall twisted walking stick. The man was dressed in heavy grey robes that seemed to flow into the shadows and mist. Liu looked the man in his eyes; the man looked straight back at him. There was no uncertainty in those eyes, only the worn expression of a man who had lived for many years.

The man tilted his head in greeting to Liu. ***"Ohayō, warrior!"*** the stranger said, his voice a soft rasp, like the crushing of dead leaves under a heavy step. "*I am Shinigami, the warden of the lost.*"

Feeling ice crawl up his spine, Liu couldn't help but feel drawn to the old man's warmth. The world seemed to fall into silence as Liu, without knowing it, stepped a little closer.

"*Why do you look so lost within these trees, yet walk with such purpose? Why are you on your way and still so adrift?*" Shinigami asked kindly, his eyes full of sympathy.

"*I'm looking for answers, and I'm heading home, so you see I know where I am going, but still feel my journey was a waste, for I am no wiser than the day I left!*" Liu replied, his voice steady despite the unease that lingered in the air. *"I wish to understand the why of it all. You seem like a man who has lived for many years and found many truths. Did you find the why of it all? The meaning of life and death?*"

With a chuckle that was tinted with thunder, Shinigami opened his mouth, words flowing like time itself. "*Young samurai, the meaning is not found in words, woods, or wounds, but in the now. Life is fleeting, death is lingering, and like all things, nothing and yet everything is change.*"

The old man talked in riddles, but despite this, Liu listened. Shinigami began to walk, gesturing for Liu to follow. They wandered deeper into the forest, where the trees stood like forgotten gravestones, ancient, untouched and unremembered. *"Tell me, what do you fear?"* Shinigami asked, his eyes narrowing.

"Not death!" Liu answered without pausing for thought. *"I fear that I will not fulfil my destiny,"* Liu admitted, a weight pressing on his chest. *"That my life will end without purpose. But how am I to know its purpose? How can one shoot an arrow without a target?"*

"Life simply is..." Shinigami replied, his voice echoing in the stillness. *"You are here, whether by design or your own will; you are here."*

As Liu spoke, the forest began to bloom around them. Vibrant colours and intense smells filled the air—things Liu had never smelled before, never seen before. A curious wonder filled him; awe plainly wrote itself across his face.

"And what of death?" Liu asked, curiosity and doubt beginning to bring him back to reality.

"Death is not..." Shinigami said, his tone reverberating with certainty. *"But the two are no different, just opposing sides of the same coin. Place a Yen upon a table, and you can only see what you can see. Try as you might, you can never see beyond its edge without physically turning it over, and once you do, you have to name the other side, just as you named the first side. Though in naming these things, you only show your lack of understanding."*

Reaching a clearing, the heavy mist sank into the ground, revealing a breathtaking tapestry of forest before them. Liu felt a sense of clarity wash over him, as if the old man's words had untied some sort of knot in his mind.

"Remember, young samurai," Shinigami said, turning to face Liu, *"Life and Death are not two; they are one. To know of one is to know of the other, and to truly live, one must understand the beauty of impermanence."*

With a knowing smile, the old man turned his back on Liu and began to walk into the trees. As he did so, he called over his shoulder to Liu.

"If one does not know the meaning of life, are they then dead? Surely, Liu, you are not dead, are you? Well, if you're not dead, then how can the dead be dead if they now, in death, know the meaning of life?"

Liu stood in the clearing, the weight of the old man's words echoing in his mind, just as theold man's words, now living, echoed through the woods.

"I COME NOT TO
STEAL, BUT TO
RECLAIM WHAT LIFE
HAS FORGOTTEN.
IN SHADOWS, I
TEACH THE LIVING
THAT LOVE'S DEPTH
CAN ONLY BE
UNDERSTOOD IN THE
SILENCE OF LOSS."

— SHINIGAMI

九

MOUNTAINS & SHOULDERS

Finally, Liu returned to the grove, the simple stretch of calm beauty that framed the hidden lake, a surreal and peaceful place that was the scene of his innermost pains. For it was here he often saw his mother's face, sitting beneath the now towering willow tree. Where once its graceful branches had sung of peace, they now seemed to whisper behind his back, to mock and ridicule him.

The picture Liu had walked into, the scene now set, was vastly different from the fragmented memories that lived within him.

Despite the years and the lessons, despite everyone else's wisdom, the opportunity and the journey,despite it all, Liu's grief was unending like the vastness of the ocean.

There were times in his life when he had found stillness and understanding.

Times when his wondering made sense, and yet deep within it all, there was this living thing he could not rid himself of.

Desperate for an outlet, for help, for something other than the consuming feeling of helplessness, Liu retreated to the willow tree.

Once there, he simply knelt, ashamed of the things inside him, his lack of true insight despite the life he had lived, the lack of fear of death, and the thirst for life. These things had not helped him.

He played the memories of some key events over in his head, replaying the meetings, the encounters, the climbs, successes and failures, and the life, simple and humble as it was, he replayed his life. He relived the happiness in moments and the anguish in what seemed like years, for nothing had been as constant as the relentless clawing and weight of the anger inside.

It wasn't just scratching; it was tearing at all that he was. The wind picked up, and as if to strike the final blow, the willow tree itself lashed out, striking Liu across the face, sharp and harsh as a razor on the wind.

Erupting, Liu struck out, aexplosion of molten rage. Eyes wide, teeth bared, his strikes were fierce and fast, the weight of his anguish adding velocity to the slashes of his well-balanced blade. Though with each slash and stab, his own balance broke; with each hack and heft, his heart sank as the uncontrolled power within him began to extinguish.

The willow did only as it could, following its own path; it danced and flowed with the restless wind. Though it was not the same as Liu, it knew the crushing realities of this place.

As it lost limb after limb, its roots sank deeper, unprepared to yield what it was.

As Liu hurled his katana at the tree, a fresh wave of anger began to bubble, for guilt now washed over him like a tsunami. The damage he had caused was terrible to behold, and all the while the willow tree sang in whispers and danced hand in hand with his own breath.

Staring at the fallen shards of the willow's long and elegant life. Branches now littered the ground. Liu watched as countless leaves finally settled upon the earth, now left lying lifeless.

Liu began to weep.

At the same time, a soft and elemental glow began to pulse from deep within the willow's core. Its remaining branches seemed to shiver and rustle, like a bird ruffling its feathers; the tree before him began to wake.

It was in that moment, as the wind softened to the lightest of breezes, Liu felt an external shift in the world as a warm, comforting weight settled over him. Deep within his mind, a presence seemed to bloom.

At first, it felt like a tiny speck; it unfurled and infused with him, it grew and reached out for him. Roots and branches and bark and leaves encircled and embraced him. There was no fear, no hesitation, and no pain as Liu heard a voice echo through him.

"I am Yanagi, and for countless years I have watched you grow. I watched you as you carried your pain, carried your burdens.

I've watched you struggle under the weight of your sword, your armour. Struggle and fight on as every thought you've held onto has grown heavier than anyone could bear."

The voice was enthralling and eternal, light and bright as it filled his body, pushed past his barriers and his self-erected walls. "*Whilst I have watched you, I have shed my leaves, embraced the chaos of the storm, and let go of shape, bending and becoming one with the world around me. Even though I have grown, roots deep and branches mighty, my weight has lessened. For I go with the world, the wind. I weep, and sag and sing in whispers."*

Yanagi's voice softened to the slightest of songs. "*Forgive the world, forgive those who hurt you, and forgive yourself! Forgive and forget, put down your past, and pick up a lighter present. This is the first step!"* Yanagi said as he withdrew from Liu's essence.

As Yanagi unfurled his damaged branches, fresh shoots began to bud and grow. As this happened, Liu tumbled through his own memories as if he were falling back into himself.

In no order, Liu's broken life unravelled in neat sections, as if written across a page.

Memory after memory, person after person flicked before him. With each page, the moments in time now clearer, somehow more tangible.

It was as if Liu had lived his whole life, taken every step with a subtle haze clouding his vision.

Still kneeling, Liu moved closer to the ancient tree. He laid his hand upon the peeling bark, hanging his head; he wept once more.

"I forgive all and accept all. For what is cannot be undone. All things are as they should be. I understand this now."

Grief and pain fell to the floor in laden drops of salt and sorrow.

"I accept the choices you made. Not only do I accept them, but I wholeheartedly forgive you, Mother!"

Soft silence sang through the clearing, but it did not hush him. For it knew he was not done. Soft as a mother's caress, the wind and willow brushed the tears from his face.

"I forgive myself, wholly and completely. I forgive myself for who, for what, and for how I am and was!"

Liu's confessions felt like a mountain lifted from his shoulders, the burden of self-inflicted pain releasing more and more with every breath.

"I COME NOT TO STEAL, BUT TO RECLAIM WHAT LIFE HAS FORGOTTEN. IN SHADOWS, I TEACH THE LIVING THAT LOVE'S DEPTH CAN ONLY BE UNDERSTOOD IN THE SILENCE OF LOSS."

— YANAGI

七

TIME & GROWTH

Yanagi had stood in this very spot for countless years, rooted deep in the earth; her branches stretched up to the sky before gracefully falling to caress the ground that gave her life.

With each new season, Yanagi was born again; her life was an endless flow—nurtured green buds of spring, the joyful emerald leaves of summer, the golden death of autumn, and the bare, graceful sleep of winter.

Through all seasons and changes, Yanagi stood fast, the silent guardian of all who sought shelter beneath her soft embrace.

Yanagi remembered one such child who had come to her, weighed down by anger and raw with pain.

She had felt the pounding of his bloody broken fists against her trunk. His rage and sorrow overflowed his tiny frame and flowed through her.

Yanagi remembered her silence as she wept alongside him, shedding tears of sticky sap.

Recalling the pain as if it were hers, she forced her roots a little deeper. As she did this, another memory washed over her. That same boy, now a man, had returned many long years later. Liu had spoken to her of promises, storms, and battles, both inside and out.

Like Yanagi, Liu had forced his roots deep, weathered all manner of storms, and journeyed through the seasons of life and death. Though this time, Liu's anger was wild and unyielding. In his anguished state, she saw into the depths of him, and Yanagi knew he needed more than time and stillness.

Though he had been shown the way and given the answers, he was so desperately, utterly, and completely lost. So, for the first time in her lifetime, she reached out to him.

When her touch had been hacked and slashed to pieces time and time again—when she saw his spirit break, Yanagi spoke.

As Liu placed his palm upon her bark, she knew she too would forgive him. For her branches would grow anew; her tears and his would nourish her own growth, just as her words and his acceptance had enabled his own growth.

As time turned, Yanagi watched many young warriors kneel before her; some alone and some in groups, kneeling within her embrace just as Liu had once done.

They trained, laughed, and grew. While some struggled, Yanagi listened, and to some, she spoke. For she knew now that the way of the willow was a rite of passage for those who studied The Ondori under Sensei Liu in the dojo that sat at the heart of Kumano.

"ALL ARE BORN FROM SEED, ALL FEEL DEATH'S PULL. WE MOURN, BUT NOT ALL FORGIVE OR FORGET. TO GROW, WE MUST LET GO OF THESE BURDENS AND SEEK NEW HEIGHTS."

— YANAGI

平

IN MEMORY OF

I had planned to write the names of my dead here, but the names are many and the pages few.

So, I will simply say thank you. For because of them, I live on.

Perhaps when I am gone, I too shall live on, unbound and always with you. If you're reading this, then you know it is true!

克

ABOUT THE AUTHOR

Louis Orozco Lopez is a Yorkshireman with Spanish and Dutch heritage, who now lives in Devon with his family. A father, husband and dreamer by day, a wordsmith by night.

COPYRIGHT

www.louisorozcolopez.com

Printed in Great Britain
by Amazon

8441e76b-2829-4376-b5df-6f9895b6796dR01